30 Ways in 30 Days

to Develop Your Relationship with

Jesus Christ

by

Minister Lynn Rentz

DEDICATION

Dedicated to my mother, Lucille Rzonca Rentz Burns who did indeed ground me as a child in developing my relationship with Father, Son, and Holy Ghost.

ACKNOWLEDGMENTS

I want to thank God first and foremost for always directing and guiding me.

Judy Leckrone thank you for planting the seed of my salvation. I thank Pastor Easton, Pastor Perry and Pastor J. Calaway for their teaching and watering the seed of my salvation.

My personal, prophetic Holy Spirit filled mentors Terry Otte, Marsha Cory and Apostle Tammy Morgan. Thank you.

And to my children, Michelle, Pamela and Edward I love you for giving me a reason to run the race.

INTRODUCTION

My name is Minister Lynn M. Rentz and I am a seeker of our heavenly Father, a follower of Jesus, and friend of the Holy Spirit. Every person is entitled to know and understand how simple it is to get past all the "religious" red tape and come to know and have a simple, loving relationship with God.

More than ever before, we are living in chaotic and stressful times. Many feel so pressed, they are reluctant to even take on anything else, or to add anything else on their plate. Religion, unfortunately, can be a pressure to someone with its agendas and requirements.

I have heard many people in the last few years say that God seems so complicated that they are afraid to even go near Him. Well, it's not God who is complicating what a loving bond could be. You see, God does not promote stress or confusion. He is just the opposite. God is all about fellowship! He wants you to succeed in life, to succeed in the very purpose for which He created you.

He wants you to understand why He sent His son Jesus to come down to earth and die on the cross. This is so you can have eternal life, and be with Him and your loved ones in heaven one day. God would love for each and every person to find themselves as a very good friend of the Holy Spirit, too.

My purpose for writing this little book is to help, in the simplest possible way, to jumpstart you to acquire a fulfilling, trusting relationship with the Lord. In this devotional, I begin each day with a scripture and end with a prayer. The scripture is for you to refer to your bible so you can get into the Word more and open up to this way of God's communication. I cannot stress how powerful His word is! The Bible is your source for knowledge, communication, promises, praise, warfare and peace. Overall, as a whole, it is your source for spiritual, emotional, and physical well-being.

My intention for the short prayer following each Scripture is to help guide you into communication with your heavenly Father. He wants us to 'be real' with Him. He wants what is in your heart to be shared with Him. Know that you can talk to God any time, and all the time.

You can start saying the prayer I have written and allow what's in your heart and spirit to take over. I can't stress how simple, yet profound, a relationship is with the Father. Religion makes it complex, but relationship eases you into true intimacy with God. As you seek to find Him with all your heart, you will. God will become a living, breathing being in your daily life..

30 Ways in 30 Days

to Develop Your Relationship with

Jesus Christ

by

Minister Lynn Rentz

Day One

> "And God saw everything that He had made
> and that it was very good."
> Genesis 1:31

God is *the* creator of the world and everything in it!
Without Him, we don't exist. If God disappeared, or did
not exist anymore, neither would we. He is our breath of
life. If He died, we would, too. He
created us for His pleasure and purposes
first and foremost. He had a plan for
you and me when we were in our
mother's womb. This plan is to give us success, and not to
do us harm.

How do I know there is a God?

How do I know that there is a God? Simply by looking at
creation all around me, I know He exists. By pursuing a

relationship with Him, He became a living being in my life. Day to day, I can speak to Him knowing that He hears me.

Through His word that was inspired by the Holy Spirit, I know He cares for me. Through His son Jesus, who died on the cross for me, I know that He loves me.

PRAYER:

Father God, I come boldly to your throne of grace today thanking you for creating me. Thank you for your love in giving me breath so I can have life. I choose to follow your plan and purpose. Increase my faith, Father, and help me to believe as it says in your word that, "we walk by faith and not by sight (2 Cor. 5:7)." Although I can't see you, I pray for your Holy Spirit to make your presence real to me. In Jesus' Name, Amen.

Day Two

"For God so loved the world, that He gave His only Son so that everyone who believes in Him will not die, but have eternal life."
John 3:16

Jesus is the umbilical cord to our Father in heaven. Without realizing just what He did on the cross for us, we cannot comprehend the love that they – the Father, Son and Holy Spirit -- have for us. Do you realize that there is no other man who ever died for an entire human race because of their sins and iniquities? Jesus was not the one who committed the crime, however He still chose to die on the cross so we can one day have eternal life with God in heaven.

> *The Cross is truly the bridge in developing a relationship with the Father.*

The cross is truly the bridge in developing a relationship

with the Father. It is necessary and only requires you to ask Jesus into your heart. In fact, let's say it together, right now:

PRAYER:

"Lord Jesus, I thank you for dying on the cross for me. I'm not sure if I can possibly fathom your love for me yet, but I realize that if I was the only human in the world you still would have tasted death on the cross for me. I want to receive your salvation now and ask you into my heart, Jesus. Although I cannot see you, it says in your word that if I only confess my sins and believe, I will be forgiven and have the gift of eternal life with you someday. I'm truly sorry and repent of anything I have done wrong. I receive your forgiveness now, in Jesus' name. Amen."

DAY 3

"However, you were taught to have a new attitude.
You were also taught to become a new person
created to be like God, truly righteous and holy."
Ephesians 4:23-24

When you receive salvation in the name of Jesus, you are a brand new creature. It says in God's word that the angels rejoice when someone accepts Jesus as their Savior.

> *God created a space inside of you to be filled by Him.*

You see, God created us for relationship with Him. He wanted us to experience His love and all the other gifts He has for us. I know of no other life that can bring us joy when we enter into a bond with the Creator.

When God created you, He made a space inside of you to

7

be filled by Him. That's your spirit. Many people never discover this and go through life feeling a void within them. They search for many different notions and potions to fill that space.

Unfortunately, the things that they are trying to fill it with only make the space larger, thereby never filling the entire void. They continue to search and keep finding more and more clutter to fill the emptiness until they finally realize that God is the only one who can bring a fullness and satisfaction that will fit and fill in the space properly.

PRAYER:

Father, thank you that you have plans for me and they include the fact that I can be a brand new creature in Christ Jesus. You even knitted a space within me to be filled by you and only you. I pray today Lord that you will guide me and help me to learn to let you in, and that I won't be swayed by "things" to fill this void within me. I pray that you will draw me unto you and teach me how to adhere and rely on you. In the name of Jesus, Amen.

Day 4

"The Lord Almighty says, "I will be your Father,
and you will be like my sons and daughters."
2 Corinthians 6:18

What do you do now after you have received God's gift of salvation? In comparison to a human relationship, you get to know the person you have already met through your heart and confession with your mouth. Now it's time to get to know the Creator: Who He is, What God likes and dislikes, What His kingdom is all about, and most importantly -- how much He loves you. It's not just about us anymore. It's about Him.

> *Getting to know your heavenly Father will help establish the bond with him.*

Getting to know your heavenly Father will help establish the bond with Him. We need to have a desire to know God and His character. Yes, God does have a character. He is the one who created personality and character. Though you cannot see Him, learning who He is through His word will help you to understand how real He is. God will continue to become more evident in your life as you continue to seek Him.

PRAYER:

Heavenly Father, I pray that you will plant within my heart the desire to know you completely. Help me not to see you as God at a distance but to understand that you are truly my Father in heaven and to know you is one way to love you. Guide me in getting to know the real You, which comes from reading Your word. Amen.

Day 5

> "Let Christ's word with all its wisdom
> and richness dwell in you."
> Colossians 3:16

Thank God that our Father gave us His word, the Bible, for continued direction, guidance, and comfort in our walk with Him and our journey in life. You can find a scripture for basically anything you are going through.

God's word is sharper than any two-edged sword. When we ground ourselves in His Word, it will become the foundation that is needed to stand on any circumstance or trial that we will encounter.

> *When we ground ourselves in His Word, it will become the foundation.*

Remember, asking Jesus into your heart and receiving forgiveness for sins is just the beginning. Now is the time to take the steps in laying out your foundation in Him.

PRAYER:

Almighty God, the seed has already been planted in my heart. I ask in the name of Jesus that I will learn to water it with your word so it will grow within me and produce the grounding that I will need to keep walking in my relationship with you and Christ. Amen.

Day 6

"But if I don't have love, I am nothing."
1 Corinthians 13:1

God wants us to remember what Jesus did on the cross for us so we can better understand the love of God. It's the love of Christ that brings others into the kingdom of God. There is a saying that has been around for years, "You catch them, Jesus will clean them."

> *It's the love of Christ that brings others into the kingdom of God.*

One of the first things we can do in our Christian walk is to show others the love of Jesus. We are to be different than those who never received the gift of salvation.

I will never forget what a friend of mine shared with me. She said the reason she wanted to know Jesus and His Kingdom better was because of the love she was shown. It wasn't giving her the do's and don'ts --- it was loving her to Christ.

Yes, discipleship is a part of growing in your journey with God, but the root of Him has to be love.

PRAYER:

Father God, I pray that your spirit will surround my heart and help me to be rooted in the love of Christ. I pray for the love to be transferred onto others. That they will see how much Jesus loved them and they will want the gift of salvation in their life also. Amen.

Day 7

"As a result, God in his kindness has given us His approval and we have become heirs who have the confidence that we have everlasting life."
Titus 3:7

How awesome to know that eternal life is included in our benefits package when we receive salvation! It's amazing to fathom how much God really loves us. Not only did He create us for His pleasure and purpose on earth, He actually wants us forever... forever and ever without end. He wants us to share in the same benefit after death comes to our physical body, namely, to remain in our spirit man with Him throughout eternity.

> *God wants us to remain with Him for eternity.*

We will one day be walking the streets of gold with our

Savior Jesus, the man who went to the cross for you and me. Though our physical body will die, our soul returns to the Creator who manufactured our very being. Praise God!

PRAYER:

Lord, It just seems to keep getting better and better, now that I have chosen to repent of my sins and invite Jesus into my heart. How awesome to think that you love me enough to want to spend eternity with me. May this truth be rooted into my heart and spirit, and give me the hope I need to continue my walk with you. Amen.

Day 8

"People die once, and after that they are judged."
Hebrews 9:27

Some say heaven is a myth. Others say it is a state of mind. Many have chosen just to believe that when we die, there is no afterlife. They say this life is all we have, and that is it.

But God's word tells us differently. We are appointed one time to die, and then be judged to determine where we will spend eternity. If we have Christ in our hearts and a relationship with Him, we will live with Him forever. But if we choose to live our life without God, we will likely end up not being able to enjoy paradise with Him.

> *It is vital to know God and be rooted in Christ.*

An example would be when someone passes away, they usually have a will. The will states that the spouse, children or possibly other relatives will be the beneficiaries. Why is that? Because they were closest to the person, they were in his or her bloodline, and they knew the person.

Though it may happen in some cases, not many people who pass away leave their legacy to complete strangers. This means it's vital to know God and be rooted in Christ, to have accepted the gift of salvation. With it comes life forever.

PRAYER:

Father, I pray today that I remain a believer through the bloodline of Jesus. Please help me to remember that it's only through Him that I have been saved and now belong to the family of God. Father thank you that you have prepared a place for me, one that I will live in forever. Amen.

Day 9

"Keep your mind clear and alert. Your opponent the devil is prowling around like a roaring lion as he looks for someone to devour." 1 Peter 5:8

In our Christian walk, we do have an adversary, an enemy both to God and to us. Satan, who was once an angel but was cast down from heaven because of his pride, hates whatever God loves. Many teachings today would have us to believe that there is no devil and there is no hell. That line of thinking, my friend, comes straight from the pit of hell.

> *We have an adversary, an enemy, both to God and to us.*

Satan is not for you, he is against you. He does not want you to have eternal life and more importantly he does not want you serving God. One of his traps is to get you to think that he does not exist so you will not have to think that you need to make a choice whether to live for God or not. But praise God!

Remember Satan was a fallen angel, not a god. His power is not equal to God. God was his maker, and one day every knee shall bow and every tongue confess that Jesus Christ is Lord….including Satan.

PRAYER:

Father God, thank you that your word states that if you are for me, who can be against me. I stand on your word today knowing that I can overcome the enemy by the power of the blood and your word. Amen.

Day 10

"However one of the soldiers stabbed Jesus's side with his
spear, and blood and water immediately came out."
John 19:34

Just what is meant by the power of the blood? Oh, there is
so much power in the blood of Jesus!   It is the blood that
cleanses us from our sins and makes us righteous in the
eyes of God.

We can also plead the blood of Jesus upon any
circumstance and situation in our
life. The blood can cleanse the
situation and protect us from the
wiles of the enemy. When we plead
the blood, we are asking and
acknowledging God to take control of the adverse
situation; to protect us from the outcome, and even to
intercede in the consequences that could have taken place.

> *We have the right
> to plead the blood
> of Jesus.*

All this requires is being a believer who has a relationship with Jesus and the Father. We have that right -- to plead the blood! Our heavenly Father will honor that.

Glory to God!

PRAYER:

Jesus, thank you for your blood that you shed on the cross and the meaning it brings to me in my relationship with you. I am grateful for the power in the blood and cherish the preciousness of it. Lord, teach me to utilize the power in the blood, knowing it cleanses all things. Amen.

Day 11

"God's word is living and active. It is sharper than any two-edged sword, and cuts as deep as the place where soul and spirit meet, the place where joint and marrow meet."
Hebrews 4:12

We also fight the enemy with the word of God. God's word is infallible. This is something I learned much, much later in my Christian walk. When I received my salvation, I read the bible so I could get to know my Creator better and understand what God wanted from me. However, I did not apply the word to my life. I simply did not grasp the fact that the word literally got sifted into my spirit man to change my heart, and to begin working to weed out the flesh.

> *Reading and speaking the word of God daily will change you from the inside out.*

God's word is alive and active. Reading it and speaking it on a daily basis will help you change from the inside out. I challenge you to find several scriptures that apply to your life right now, whether it's for finances, health, more joy, fear, sadness, or whatever situation you are facing.

When God created the earth, He spoke and it came to pass. Allow the Holy Spirit to root His words deep down within you. Say them with faith. Believe that it will come to pass because God's word says He is not a liar, and that He watches over His word to perform it.

PRAYER:

Father, I speak your word into my life right now. Thank you that I can be changed through it, as well as changing my circumstances and situations that I'm going through. There is nothing that cannot be changed when I apply your word to my life. May my faith water what I am planting within my heart. Amen.

Day 12

"Faith convinces us that God created the world through His word. That means what can be seen was made by something that could not be seen."
Hebrews 11:3

Learning to water your spirit with the word of God sometimes takes time. It is not an overnight process. We need to keep developing our faith in our heavenly Father.

> **Speak God's word with life, faith and expectancy.**

Faith goes hand in hand with the word of God. If you just repeat scriptures all day long without believing that it will come to pass, probably nothing will come to pass.

God's word should be spoken with life, with expectancy, with faith, knowing that your heavenly Father wants to give you good things and help you in all trials that you will face. Allow that word to become energized within you! If He spoke it, He will do it!

PRAYER:

Lord, give me the patience to allow your word to take place in my life. Help me not to grow weary, tired, or faint. Cover me with your joy while your word is growing within me. Amen.

Day 13

"It is good to announce your mercy in the morning
and your faithfulness in the evening."
Psalms 92:2

Beginning your day with the scripture, "This is the day that
the Lord has made, let us be glad and rejoice in it (Psalm
118:24)," can set the tone for your day. Though we may
experience some "bad hair days", beginning your day with a
word from the Bible will communicate to God that you
want Him to bless your day and be
a part of it.

> **Begin your day
> with a word from
> the Bible .**

It's sometimes hard to even want
to wake up when you are going
through trials and "stuff". Making the Creator a part of
your day can ease your mind and spirit, knowing that, "All
things work together to the good of those who love God
and are called according to His purpose (Romans 8:28)."

PRAYER:

Father God, please help me today to know and understand that your love, care, and grace are there for the taking. May I remember to start each day with prayer and your word, inviting your presence into all areas of my life. Amen.

Day 14

"God didn't spare His own Son, but handed him over to death for all of us."
Romans 8:32

Grace is undeserved merit, or favor, a wonderful thing that we receive from God.

Remember when you were growing up as a child, and would be playing outside with your friends? You were having so much fun that you asked if you could stay out longer? My parents called it a "grace period". I didn't do anything to deserve it. Once in a while I may have been on my best behavior to earn it, but most of the time it was just given to me!

> God's gift of grace is free. We can't buy it or earn it.

God's gift of grace is free. We can't buy it or do anything

to earn it. It's just one of God's benefits that, once again, comes with the package of having salvation in Christ.

PRAYER:

Jesus, thank you for grace. I know that there is nothing I can do to earn it. I receive your grace and ask that you give me what I need for today. Amen.

Day15

"The one who loves us gives us an overwhelming victory in all these difficulties."
Romans 8:37

God's grace is also sufficient for all we encounter and face. That's what His word states. Though we walk a path to seek God deeper, we will always have trials and things to overcome. That's where God's grace comes in.

Life is not always easy, but now you have someone watching your back. You now have a hope in the midst of the storm. You now have an answer in the middle of the night. You can now see light in the darkened room.

> *God's grace is sufficient.*

Jesus promised to never leave you nor forsake you. He will give you what you need to get through the rough times.

PRAYER:

Father, I cry out for your grace for all I am going through right now in my life. Your word says your grace is sufficient for me. Help me this day to abide in your grace in Jesus's name. Amen.

Day 16

> "The disciples were overcome with fear and
> asked each other, 'Who is this man? Even
> the wind and the sea obey Him!' "
> Mark 4:41

Why do we pray in the name of Jesus? We pray in the
name of Jesus because His name is above all other names.
When we stand up against the enemy, and the enemy flees
from us, it's not us of whom he is afraid. It's what backs us
up: the Name of Jesus.

Pray in the Name of Jesus.

Satan knows he is a defeated foe. He
knows what Jesus did on the cross by
disarming the principalities and taking
back the keys to life and death.

When we accept Jesus as our Savior and Master, we have
the right to use His name to back up God's word and fight

the enemy.

When you pray and give your requests to God, always pray in the name of Jesus. He is our chief intercessor.

PRAYER:

Heavenly Father, in the name of Jesus I come before you today acknowledging Your Son as my Savior and Master. Thank you for yet another benefit that we have received because of the precious blood that was shed by Jesus Christ. Amen.

Day 17

"Never worry about anything, but in every situation
let God know what you need in prayers and
requests while giving thanks."
Philippians 4:6

When one becomes a follower of Jesus, one can tend to
think that he might not ever have any problems again.
However, that's not the case. The only group of people on
earth who don't have any difficulties are usually six feet
underground.

I came to that realization very quickly. Sometimes it
seemed as if I had **more** battles to
face. I quickly learned that Pastors,
Teachers, and other ministers
working for God did not lead
"perfect lives" -- lives that never

> *You don't have to
> face your
> challenges alone.*

met with opposition, personal trials and storms.

They too encountered obstacles, disappointment and "stuff". However, they knew that they had to continue their walk by studying God's word and applying it to their lives. This way they could become the overcomer for whom Christ had gone to the cross.

The wonderful part about being a follower of Jesus is that you don't have to face your challenges alone anymore. You can give them to God and ask for help. He wants us to rely on Him, to adhere to Him and cling to Him.

PRAYER:

Thank you God that you actually want to help me in my daily struggles. I am grateful that I have a friend in Jesus and He intercedes for me. I give you what I can't control to handle, because you can control any circumstance and problem I'm facing. In Jesus' name. Amen.

Day 18

"Trust the Lord and do good things."

Psalms 37:3

Trust is one of the most important elements in our walk with the Father. It's sometimes not easy developing that trust in Him. We want to do things our way when we have to make a decision or when we encounter a situation we have to go through.

It's human nature to want to be in control and make sure we are the one in the driver's seat at all times. But God wants us to trust Him. He wants us to develop our faith in Him and in His almighty power.

> **Learn to trust God in all things.**

Sometimes we don't understand why things happen, but when we look back, we can realize that He did have it all under control working out all things for our good. After all

He already knows the outcome.

PRAYER:

Heavenly Father, Increase my faith, my faith in you, and my trust in You. I pray that I will learn how to rely on You, for You know what's best for me and my circumstance. I give you my permission to help me in whatever ways I need help. Thank you Father that I can cast my cares upon You. In Jesus's name. Amen.

Day 19

"But thank God, though you were once slaves of sin, you have become obedient with all your heart to the standard of teaching in which you were instructed and to which you were committed."
Romans 6:17

Your walk with Jesus is not just about a bunch of "do's and don'ts". If the gospel was presented that way, no one would want to live for Christ. Instead, Christianity should begin with love. The love of God gets planted in our hearts, weeding out all the junk and covering us with its healing power.

> *We now accept responsibility to walk like Jesus.*

However, the more we walk in God's word, we begin to learn the kind of character we need to develop. When we take Jesus into our heart, the seed is planted. We now accept the responsibility to try to walk like Jesus did. To do that, we must change our thinking from the inside first.

When we change our thinking from the inside first, the outside will change also. It is making our flesh line up with our spirit, instead of the other way around. Our spirit man indeed wants to do good, but it's our flesh that we have to fight daily.

PRAYER:

Father God, help me to put off the works of my flesh and implement the fruits of the Holy Spirit: Love, Peace, Joy, Goodness, Faithfulness, Meekness, Patience, Gentleness and Self-control. Give me the desire to live by the Spirit and to desire God's will for my life. Allow me to witness about God's love to others and go about doing good as Jesus did. Amen.

Day 20

"After Jesus was baptized, He immediately came up from
the water.   Suddenly the heavens were opened, and He saw
the Spirit of God coming down as a dove to Him."
Matthew 3:16

The Holy Spirit should be a living, breathing, active part of
your daily walk. You need the Holy Spirit to enable you to
walk the walk and talk the talk. He is our counselor,
friend, comforter and guide. He was given to us by the
Father when Jesus went up into heaven.

> *You need the
> Holy Spirit to
> walk the walk.*

When we get baptized by being
immersed in water after we receive
Jesus, we have been given the infinite power of the Holy
Spirit, making it easier to walk with Him. Daily, we can

41

expect to encounter all kinds of temptation, cravings and desires that are not good for us, but we have the Holy Spirit to help us. He will guide us and comfort us when we ask and do our part.

PRAYER:

Holy Spirit, please be a part of my life. Help me to get to know you. Enable me to walk the daily path as a follower of Christ. Bless me with wisdom in all areas of my life. Show me the things I need to change within me and help me to make that change. Amen.

Day 21

"In the last days, God says, "I will pour out my
Spirit on everyone. Your sons and daughters
will speak what God has revealed. Young men
will see visions. Your old men will dream
dreams. In those days I will pour out my
Spirit on my servants, both men and women.
They will speak what God has revealed."
Acts 2:17

Every day when you get up and make time for your
heavenly Father, always acknowledge the Holy Spirit and
ask Him to be a part of your day.
The Holy Spirit can provide the
wisdom and counsel you need in all
areas of your life. The Holy Spirit
wants you to succeed just as God
does. He cares about your job, finances, business and
relationships, just to name a few. He cares about all that

> *Ask the Holy
> Spirit to be a part
> of your day.*

pertains to you and your life.

When you get to know the Holy Spirit it will become natural to you that He is with you. His presence will become gloriously real to you.

PRAYER:

Holy Spirit, thank you that you want to be my friend, counselor and help. I invite you from this moment on into all areas of my life. Touch my mind and heart with your counsel and soundness. Amen.

Day 22

"You make the path of life known to me. Complete joy is in your presence. Pleasures are by your side forever." Psalms 16:11

One of the most powerful scriptures in the bible to overcome any negative emotion or situation is, "The joy of the Lord is my strength (Psalm 28:7)."

God wants us to realize that there is a difference between joy and happiness. Happiness is temporary and depends on the circumstance, environment or situation. Joy is that full feeling in our heart and spirit knowing that, regardless of any trial we are experiencing, we are still His.

> *Learn to tap into the joy of Christ.*

We are His children and we have a God who sits upon the throne. You belong to the Creator of this world. His Son Jesus is King of Kings and Lord of Lords. He is our breath of life and will continue to love us unconditionally forever and ever.

When you learn to tap into the joy of Christ, it will become a very strong weapon in the down times.

PRAYER:

Father, in the name of Jesus, I pray for your joy. I ask the Holy Spirit to bestow upon my heart the joy of the Lord. I believe in your word that it will be my strength knowing there is nothing that can separate me from the love of Christ. Amen.

Day 23

"Sing a new song to the Lord, because He has done marvelous things." Psalms 98:1

Another weapon that we believers have been given is the spirit of praise. God inhabits the praises of His people, and it is just a good thing to worship God and give Him praise. The enemy can't stand hearing praise and God's children singing songs to Him.

Praise can break down the walls of oppression and depression. There is such a spirit of release, comfort and joy when you begin to praise God for Who He is.

Your praise is a weapon.

Invest in a praise CD! Memorize songs you heard in a church. If you don't attend or don't have access to a church right now, open up your bible to the book of Psalms and add a melody to them. Yes! Sing the Psalms!

When you begin to feel fear, sadness, tension and other negative feelings and emotions, turn up the praise!

PRAYER:

Hallelujah, Father God! I praise you for who you are! You are my God and my King! May my mouth be filled continually with your praise. I bless your holy name Father in the name of Jesus! Rejoice my King in what You hear! May it be a sweet, sweet sound in your ear! Amen.

Day 24

"It is good to give thanks to the Lord, to make music to praise Your name, O Most High."
Psalms 92:1

Praise Him in the morning, noon and night! Don't forget to praise God in the good times, also. When life is going good, take the time to fellowship with Him on a daily basis. He wants a living, breathing, relationship with you at all times. Not just in the good times or the bad, but in ALL times.

> *Praise God in the morning, noon and night.*

Praise brings the presence of God into your prayer time with Him. God loves it when we remember all His wondrous deeds and blessings. Praising Him, too, for someone else's blessings probably gives God great pleasure. Take time to thank Him when someone else you know gets blessed.

PRAYER:

Jesus, I praise and thank you today. Thank you for what you have done so far in my life, and thank you for what you are going to do. I ask that the Holy Spirit will enable me to nurture my relationship with God on an every day basis. Amen.

Day 25

"All the believers kept meeting together, and they shared everything with each other." Acts 2:44

One of the things that God wants us to do is to gather with other believers in the assembly. This means it is good to choose to go to a bible-believing church, attend biblical studies or ministry gatherings.

We not only give glory and honor to our heavenly Father with other believers, but we reap the benefits of growing in the knowledge of God and His word when we are able to hear it being preached. It's good to fellowship with other believers and God does inhabit the praises of His people.

> *Assemble with other believers in a gathering place.*

Some say that many who attend church or biblical

gatherings can be hypocrites and not followers of Christ. Again, that's why its important to have the relationship and the act of salvation . Having Jesus in your heart will always be the inward testimony.

PRAYER:

Father, I thank you that you provide another way for us to grow closer to you through the assembly with other believers. I pray Lord that you will give me ears to hear and the ability to do what your word says as its being preached to my heart. Amen.

Day 26

"We need to hold on to our declaration of faith. We have a
superior chief priest who has gone through the heavens.
That person is Jesus, the Son of God."
Hebrews 4:14

If you are wondering what church to attend, you need to
plant yourself in a bible-believing church and/or ministry
that preaches and teaches the word of God. That's why it's
important to read the word and make the Holy Spirit your
friend, so you will hear and discern where God wants you.

> *All gods are not created equal. There is only one true God: Jesus.*

All gods are not created equal.
There is only one true God that
sent His only Son Jesus to die for
our sins. There may be other good prophets and teachers
that lived on this earth, but only one man died for all
mankind. His name is Jesus Christ, and He died and rose
again so we can have eternal life with the Father.

PRAYER:

Father God, I ask that you will lead me to a church or ministry where You want me to go. Please open doors for me so I can make this a part of my walk with You. Help me to grasp the importance of hearing Your word from a man or woman of God. Amen.

Day 27

"Bring one-tenth of your income into the
storehouse so that there may be food in My house.
Test me in this way, says the Lord of Armies. See if
I won't open the windows of heaven for you and
flood you with blessings."
Malachi 3:10

There are many controversies and arguments about the
issue of tithing. In case you don't know what tithing is, it is
the principle of giving back to God ten percent of what we
make, or what the bible calls the first fruits.

> *Give to God's house and He will take care of yours.*

I have heard many people go back
and forth on this principle. Some
have called churches and pastors thieves because they are
giving "their money" to ministries for the kingdom of God.
Let it be known that giving money to a bible based

foundational church or ministry has brought many to Christ through people's tithes and offerings.

We are supposed to give to God's kingdom. There are many references in God's word about planting seed and reaping a harvest. We can expect God to take care of us when we take care of His kingdom.

PRAYER:

Father, guide me in your word to understand more about this principle of giving. Please open my heart and spirit. Rid me of mindsets that have kept me from understanding, and in fact have kept me in fear of, giving to your kingdom. In Jesus name. Amen.

Day 28

"Be careful that you don't forget the Lord your God." Deuteronomy 8:11

To further the principle of tithing, it is simply a covenant between you and God. You are giving a portion back to God to further His kingdom and also proving to Him that you trust Him to meet all your needs.

It's not always easy to start tithing. Satan will be the first to try and stop you, because he even knows you cannot out-give God. Then there will be the others who will tell you that so and so is rich because he is taking money from his or her congregation. Some may even try and convince you that tithing is from the Old Testament only, and is not expected for today.

> *Tithing is a covenant between you and God.*

But I can tell you this from my own personal covenant with

God….He does keep His word and watches over it to perform it. I know that I could have had worse situations happen in my life financially had I not been trusting in God as my overall provider.

Pray always where God wants you to give your seed – your tithe. If you are attending a church or ministry, it's always good to give where you are getting fed, meaning receiving the word. Offerings also are pleasing to God. Offerings are sacrificial giving above the tithe.

PRAYER:

Father, I pray that you will provide for me the provision to begin tithing and giving to your kingdom to further your gospel. Show me Father and help me to remember that I am doing this unto you and you will take care of me in all ways. Amen

Day 29

> "Imitate God since you are the children He loves.
> Live in love as Christ also loved us."
> Ephesians 5:1

Serving God is another area that a Christian should be open to in his or her life. Not everyone will be called to be a pastor, a minister in a church setting, a missionary or a field minister.

However, Jesus Christ has called everyone who follows

> **Jesus has called everyone to do something.**

Him to do something. It could be spreading the good news about Jesus to the fellow down the street, giving hope to someone who feels that he has nothing left for which to live. Or you could be led to share your testimony at the workplace.

God can use you to minister His gospel to your friends, family and even strangers. God will joyfully answer your prayer when you ask Him what you are called to do. Pray for the Spirit of God to guide you into all truth.

PRAYER:

Father, I pray in the name of Jesus that you will direct me where I need to go and reveal my purpose that you have for me. Place in my heart the desire to serve you and bring others into your kingdom. Amen.

Day 30

There is no one like You among the gods, O Lord, Nor are there any works like Yours. All nations whom You have made shall come and worship before You, O Lord, And they shall glorify Your name. For You are great and do wondrous deeds; You alone are God.
Psalms 86:8-10

God is a great God! Remember whom you serve! He is able! Nothing is impossible with Him and all things are possible with Him. He can make a way where there is no other way.

> *Remember whom you serve. Nothing is impossible with God.*

He loves you with an everlasting love. Jesus took all of our infirmities when He went to the cross. There is nothing that you cannot do without the power and presence of your heavenly Father.

You need to recognize on a daily basis just what Jesus did for you on that cross. Always remember on a daily basis just how much God, your Father, loves you.

PRAYER:

Father God, I thank you today that I serve the one true God...the God of the impossible and Creator of all things. I thank you for the love of Jesus and the miracle of eternal life with you one day. Amen.

ABOUT THE AUTHOR:

Minister Lynn M. Rentz was born in Evergreen Park, Illinois and has resided in Indiana for most of her life. Ever since she was ten years old, she knew she wanted to help others and serve God somehow. Throughout the years she has personally ministered to many individuals that God has placed in her life.

This past June of 2014, she has become an ordained pastor and minister of the gospel. Along with her life experience, and sitting under the mentorship of pastors, teachers, and prophetic men and women of God, she has now started her own ministry.

I Care Outreach Ministries has been formed to reach out to those who are desiring a deeper walk with the Lord and also to those who want to know how to develop a relationship with Jesus Christ. Her outreach includes prayer, teaching, and spiritual care. She believes in healing and deliverance for the abused, unloved, and those that feel unworthy. Their ministry also is connected with those who minister in prisons and also with victims of human trafficking.

For more information on Minister Lynn's outreach, you can email her at icareoutreach@yahoo.com or check out her Facebook page "I Care Outreach Ministry".

www.ingramcontent.com/pod-product-compliance
Lightning Source LLC
Chambersburg PA
CBHW060423050426
42449CB00009B/2101